D1490459

MONSTERS!

SEA CREATURES

PETER CASTELLANO

HOT TOPICS

Gareth Stevens
PUBLISHING

Please visit our website, www.garethstevens.com. For a free color catalog of all our high-quality books, call toll free 1-800-542-2595 or fax 1-877-542-2596.

Cataloging-in-Publication Data

Castellano, Peter.
Sea creatures / by Peter Castellano.
p. cm. — (Monsters!)
Includes index.
ISBN 978-1-4824-4091-1 (pbk.)
ISBN 978-1-4824-4092-8 (6-pack)
ISBN 978-1-4824-4093-5 (library binding)
1. Sea monsters — Juvenile literature. I. Castellano, Peter. II. Title.
QL89.2.S4 C38 2016
591.77—d23

First Edition

Published in 2016 by
Gareth Stevens Publishing
111 East 14th Street, Suite 349
New York, NY 10003

Designer: Samantha DeMartin
Editor: Kristen Nelson

Photo credits: Background iulias/Shutterstock.com; text frame Dmitry Natashin/Shutterstock.com; caption boxes Azuzl/Shutterstock.com; cover, p. 1 Fer Gregory/Shutterstock.com; p. 5 mj007/Shutterstock.com; p. 7 Victor Habbick/Shutterstock.com; p. 7 (map) ekler/Shutterstock.com; p. 9 ullstein bild/ullstein bild/Getty Images; p. 11 Keystone/Hulton Archive/Getty Images; p. 13 pulaw/Flickr.com; p. 15 Esteban De Armas/Shutterstock.com; p. 17 CM Dixon/Hulton Archive/Getty Images; p. 19 David Doubilet/National Geographic/Getty Images; p. 21 pavila/Shutterstock.com; pp. 23, 30 (blue whale, liopleurodon, mosasaur) Michael Rosskothen/Shutterstock.com; p. 25 Frederic Lewis/Archive Photos/Getty Images; p. 27 Andreas Meyer/Shutterstock.com; p. 29 Ministry of Fisheries/Getty Images News/Getty Images; p. 30 (mola) Mohamed Tazi Cherti/Shutterstock.com.

Printed in the United States of America

CPSIA compliance information: Batch #CW16GS: For further information contact Gareth Stevens, New York, New York at 1-800-542-2595.

CONTENTS

MYSTERIOUS WATER

he constant movement of a ody of water can easily make wave look like the back of uge water monster! **Myths** bout sea **creatures** have been art of **cultures** all over the orld for thousands of years. ould some of them be true?

BEYOND THE MYTH

According to the National Oceanic and
Atmospheric Administration, we've only explored
less than 5 percent of the ocean!

NESSIE

Of the many mysterious deep, dark waters on Earth, none is more mysterious than Loch Ness in Scotland. That's because it's said to be home to the most famous mythical sea creature—Nessie, the Loch Ness monster.

LOCH NESS

SCOTLAND

BEYOND THE MYTH

"Loch" is the Scottish word for lake. Loch Ness is 754 feet (230 m) deep at its deepest point!

Written reports of a monster in Loch Ness date back as far as AD 565! The myth most people know came from a report made in 1933. The local newspaper wrote about the sighting—and a monster was born.

BEYOND THE MYTH

More sightings followed the first. Lots of money was offered to the person who could catch the Loch Ness monster soon after!

9

In 1934, a doctor produced a photograph of a huge sea creature he claimed was Nessie. It was in the newspaper, and most people thought it was real. However, in 1994, it was discovered that the photo had been faked!

BEYOND THE MYTH

The 1934 photograph of Nessie isn't the only fake **evidence**. One man used a stuffed hippopotamus foot to make monster tracks around Loch Ness!

KELPIES

Nessie may have grown from another Scottish sea creature myth. Kelpies, or water horses, are water spirits that can change shapes. They mostly take the form of a cow or pony and drag people into the water to drown!

BEYOND THE MYTH

Kelpie myths state that once someone has hopped
on the kelpie to.ride it, they can't get off!

THE KRAKEN

Part of Scandinavian myth, the monstrous Kraken was said to be so large, sailors mistook its body for an island! The Kraken was truly thought to be real. It was part of science books about animals in the 1700s!

BEYOND THE MYTH

The Kraken and its giant **tentacles** were memorably shown in the 2006 movie *Pirates of the Caribbean: Dead Man's Chest.*

IN GREEK MYTH

Greek writer Homer featured two frightening sea monsters in his story the *Odyssey*. They lived along a narrow waterway the hero, Odysseus, and his ship had to pass through. Scylla had six heads and three rows of sharp teeth!

BEYOND THE MYTH

In Greek art, Scylla had a fish's tail and dogs coming out of the front of her body.

Charybdis drank and threw up all the water in the waterway three times a day. This was terrible for ships trying to travel through! Most likely, this sea monster was the Greeks' explanation of the fast-moving, circular waters of a whirlpool.

BEYOND THE MYTH

In another Greek myth, a hero named Perseus kills Cetus, a huge sea monster controlled by the sea god Poseidon.

AZTEC EARTH EATER

The Aztec people believed that the universe formed from the body of a sea monster named Cipactli. Sometimes Cipactli was said to look like a crocodile or somewhat like a fish. The stories agree, though—Cipactli had unending hunger!

BEYOND THE MYTH

The Aztec believed their gods first made water.
Then, they made Cipactli to live in the water.

When the gods were making Earth, Cipactli kept eating what they made! So, they pulled apart the monster's body to free the universe from it. The gods then made parts of Cipactli's body the heavens, Earth, and underworld.

BEYOND THE MYTH

Cipactli was able to eat so much because it had
extra mouths all over its body!

THE BIBLE AND BEYOND

The Leviathan is an ancient sea creature from myths around the Middle East. It's part of Jewish mythology as a large sea snake, and it's also in the Bible! The Leviathan is said to breathe fire hot enough to make the ocean boil.

BEYOND THE MYTH

The Leviathan's skin is so strong, swords can't cut it.

25

REAL SEA MONSTERS!

Huge sea creatures that sound like monsters have lived in Earth's waters—and still do. Plesiosaurs swam in many bodies of water about 200 million years ago! They had long necks and four flippers.

BEYOND THE MYTH

Plesiosaurs were reptiles, meaning they had scales, were cold-blooded, and laid eggs.

27

The kraken isn't real, but something much like it is. The giant squid has eight arms and two tentacles, giving it a total length of more than 40 feet (12 m)! Its eyes are as big as a person's head.

BEYOND THE MYTH

If you think the giant squid is monstrous, the colossal squid will surely scare you! It may be even bigger than the giant squid.

COLOSSAL SQUID

29

Monstrously Huge Sea Creatures

MOSASAURS

Mosasaurs were the top predator when they lived in Earth's seas more than 66 million years ago. They could reach 56 feet (17 m) long and weigh 22 tons (20 mt).

BLUE WHALES

Blue whales are likely the largest animals that have ever lived on Earth! Their hearts weigh as much as a car.

LIOPLEURODONS

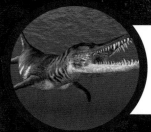

Liopleurodons lived between 150 million and 165 million years ago and were fast swimmers. They looked as dangerous as they were to the fish and squids they hunted. Liopleurodons had a large head with lots of big teeth!

MOLAS

Molas, or ocean sunfish, are the heaviest bony fish swimming on Earth today. They can weigh almost 5,000 pounds (2,268 kg)!

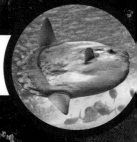

Could these huge, real creatures have been the cause of some sea monster myths?

FOR MORE INFORMATION

BOOKS

Lassieur, Allison. *Is the Loch Ness Monster Real?* Mankato, MN: Amicus, 2016.

Peebles, Alice. *Monsters of the Gods.* Minneapolis, MN: Lerner 2016.

WEBSITES

Sea Monster Facts

bbc.co.uk/sn/prehistoric_life/dinosaurs/seamonsters/
Read about many sea animals that no longer exist—but still seem quite monstrous!

Sea Monsters

amnh.org/exhibitions/past-exhibitions/mythic-creatures/
water-creatures-of-the-deep/sea-monsters
The American Museum of Natural History describes many sea monsters, both real and mythical.

GLOSSARY

creature: any type of animal

culture: the beliefs and ways of life of a group of people

evidence: something that helps show or disprove the truth of something

myth: a legend or story

tentacle: a long, thin body part that sticks out from an animal's head or mouth

INDEX